Summersdale Publishers Ltd
46 West Street
Chichester
West Sussex
PO19 1RP
UK

www.summersdale.com

Printed and bound in China

ISBN: 978-1-84953-592-2

Substantial discounts on bulk quantities of Summersdale books are available to corporations, professional associations and other organisations. For details contact Nicky Douglas by telephone: +44 (0) 1243 756902, fax: +44 (0) 1243 786300 or email: nicky@summersdale.com.

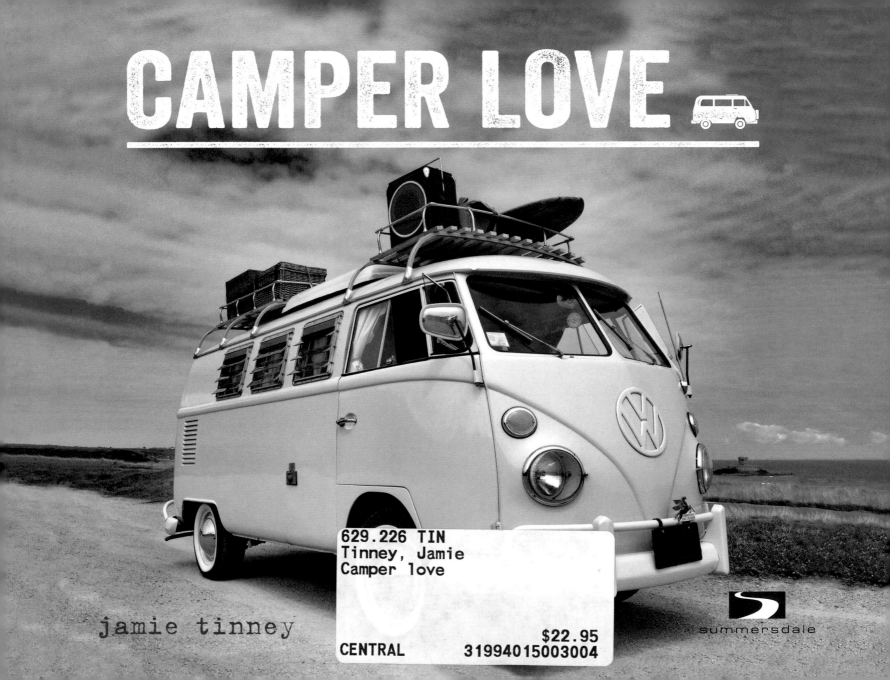

CAMPER LOVE

jamie tinney

Introduction

When the last VW Type 2 Kombi van rolled off the production line on 31 December 2013, it marked the end of an era of style. The camper van wasn't just for travelling from A to B, it was about quality of life, providing its owner with the opportunity to set off and follow wherever their dreams may take them — and with little preparation, apart from a kettle and provisions for that essential roadside cuppa for when you (and, most likely, your camper van) need to take a breather.

Anyone who owns — or aspires to own — one of these vehicles will tell you that they add up to far more than the sum of their physical parts. The Dub's wide-set headlights give it a friendly looking face; the doors often require a special knack to close; the pop-top allows you to stand up in the back and stretch after a comfortable sleep in the middle of nowhere. With only the birds and a breathtaking view for company, your camper is a place to grill those sausages and huddle together for warmth when the barbeque is rained off.

Camper Love is a heartfelt homage to the VW van, loved by free spirits, happy holidaymakers and classic car enthusiasts from every walk of life. So get comfortable and prepare to be transported (albeit slowly) down memory lane.

'Simplicity is
the ultimate
sophistication...'

WILLIAM GADDIS

'Do not dwell on the past; do not dream of the future; concentrate the mind on the present moment.'

BUDDHA

AFTER IMPORTING THIS VAN FROM CALIFORNIA, THE OWNERS FOUND THREE BULLET HOLES IN ITS FRONT END. THEY DECIDED TO NAME IT MARVIN, AFTER THE CHARACTER IN *PULP FICTION*, WHOSE FACE ALSO MET WITH THE BUSINESS END OF A GUN.

'Beauty is in the eye of the beholder.'

MARGARET WOLFE HUNGERFORD

AN OLD PANEL VAN IN NEED OF SOME LOVE

'The open road is a beckoning, a strangeness, a place where a man can lose himself.'

WILLIAM LEAST HEAT-MOON

'In all things of nature
there is something of
the marvellous.'

ARISTOTLE

LITTLE COUGH, NAMED AFTER A SHORT STORY BY DYLAN THOMAS

'Dare to be different.'

'Fashion fades, only style remains the same.'

COCO CHANEL

'Remember that the most valuable antiques are dear old friends.'

H. JACKSON BROWN JR

1978 WESTFALIA WAITING FOR SPRING

'Not all those who wander are lost.'

J. R. R. TOLKIEN

'There are far better things ahead than any we leave behind.'

C. S. LEWIS

'One's destination is never a place, but a new way of seeing things.'

HENRY MILLER

'Without craftsmanship, inspiration is a mere reed shaken in the wind.'

JOHANNES BRAHMS

PUMBA, OWNED AND RESTORED WITH LOVE BY DOUG AND LOUISE PHILLIPS

'May your trails be crooked, winding... leading to the most amazing view.'

EDWARD ABBEY

'Have no fear of perfection.'

SALVADOR DALÍ

'There was nowhere to go but everywhere, keep rolling under the stars...'

JACK KEROUAC

'The difference between something good and something great is attention to detail.'

CHUCK SWINDOLL

'Blessed are the curious for they shall have adventures.'

LOVELLE DRACHMAN

'The goal isn't to
live forever, the
goal is to create
something that will.'

CHUCK PALAHNIUK

'Life is to be enjoyed, not just endured.'

GORDON B. HINCKLEY

'In order to be irreplaceable one must always be different.'

COCO CHANEL

A HIGHLY MODIFIED CAMPER WHICH PRODUCES OVER 600 BHP –
PROBABLY THE QUICKEST CAMPER IN THE UK

'Style is a way to say who you are without having to speak.'

RACHEL ZOE

'Friendship isn't about whom you've known the longest... It's about who came, and never left your side...'

ANONYMOUS

'A good style must have an air of novelty, at the same time concealing its art.'

ARISTOTLE

'I would rather wake up in the middle of nowhere than in any city on earth.'

STEVE MCQUEEN

'Most of my treasured memories of travel are recollections of sitting.'

ROBERT THOMAS ALLEN

'A good holiday is one spent among people whose notions of time are vaguer than yours.'

J. B. PRIESTLEY

A WEDDING CAR, CORNISH STYLE

'It is quality rather than quantity that matters.'

SENECA THE YOUNGER

'The human spirit needs places where nature has not been rearranged by the hand of man.'

RALPH WALDO EMERSON

'How far is my journey and
how little is the provision
I have.'

AL-FUDAYL IBN 'LYAD

'A good traveller has no fixed plans, and is not intent on arriving.'

LAO TZU

'My dreams are tangled in images of stars and clouds and firelight.'

JOHN GEDDES

1978 DEVON MOONRAKER IN MARINO YELLOW. HUGH AND SHIRLEY SEARLE ARE THE
SECOND OWNERS AND BOUGHT IT IN 1995. IT IS A DAILY RUNNER AND HOLIDAY HOME

'The sea, once it's cast its spell, holds one in its net forever.'

JACQUES COUSTEAU

'Luxury is in each detail.'

HUBERT DE GIVENCHY

'Grace is the beauty
of form under the
influence of freedom.'

FRIEDRICH SCHILLER

'We do not remember
days, we remember
moments.'

CESARE PAVESE

'People will stare. Make it worth their while.'

HARRY WINSTON

'It's the little details that are vital. Little things make big things happen...'

JOHN WOODEN

'He who would travel happily must travel light.'

ANTOINE DE SAINT-EXUPÉRY

'It is good to have
an end to journey
towards, but it is
the journey that
matters in the end.'

URSULA K. LE GUIN

'Where thou art – that
– is home.'

EMILY DICKINSON

FLORENCE, A 1978 BAY WESTIE, PICTURED IN A CAMPSITE IN SUNNY HAMBURG

'Truly elegant design incorporates top-notch functionality into a simple, uncluttered form.'

DAVID LEWIS

'Half the fun of travel is the aesthetic of lostness.'

RAY BRADBURY

1978 WESTFALIA CAMPMOBILE IN LEWIS AND CLARK STATE PARK, WASHINGTON

'Explore, Dream, Discover.'

'Riches do not consist in the possession of treasures, but in the use made of them.'

'Thousands of tired, nerve-shaken, over-civilised people are beginning to find out that wilderness is a necessity.'

JOHN MUIR

1967 CALIFORNIAN WESTFALIA AT ST OUEN'S BAY, JERSEY

'I restore myself
when I'm alone.'

MARILYN MONROE

FLOWER POWER AT A VW MEETING IN FLEY, BURGUNDY

'Freedom lies in being bold.'

ROBERT FROST

'I don't know where I'm going, but I'm on my way.'

CARL SAGAN

WESTFALIA AT MAGDALEN ISLANDS, QUEBEC, CANADA

'Wherever you are, be all there.'

JIM ELLIOT

HOT CHILLI, 1971 BAY WINDOW

'Form and function should
be one.'

'There is pleasure
in the pathless
woods, There is
rapture on the
lonely shore...'

LORD BYRON

'Travelling's not something you're good at. It's something you do. Like breathing.'

GAYLE FOREMAN

'Everything has beauty but not everyone sees it.'

CONFUCIUS

'But what is happiness except the simple harmony between a man and the life he leads?'

ALBERT CAMUS

'Decorating is about... creating a quality of life, a beauty that nourishes the soul.'

ALBERT HADLEY

'The beauty you see in me
is a reflection of you.'

VANNA BONTA

'Rare is the union of beauty and purity.'

JUVENAL

'Live in the sunshine, swim in the sea, drink in the wild air.'

Calling all camper lovers...

Do you have an eye for a perfect pop-top or a beautiful bay?
If so, we'd like to hear from you!
Send in your own shots of beautiful camper vans to be in with a
chance of featuring in the next instalment of *Camper Love*.

Mail to:
auntie@summersdale.com

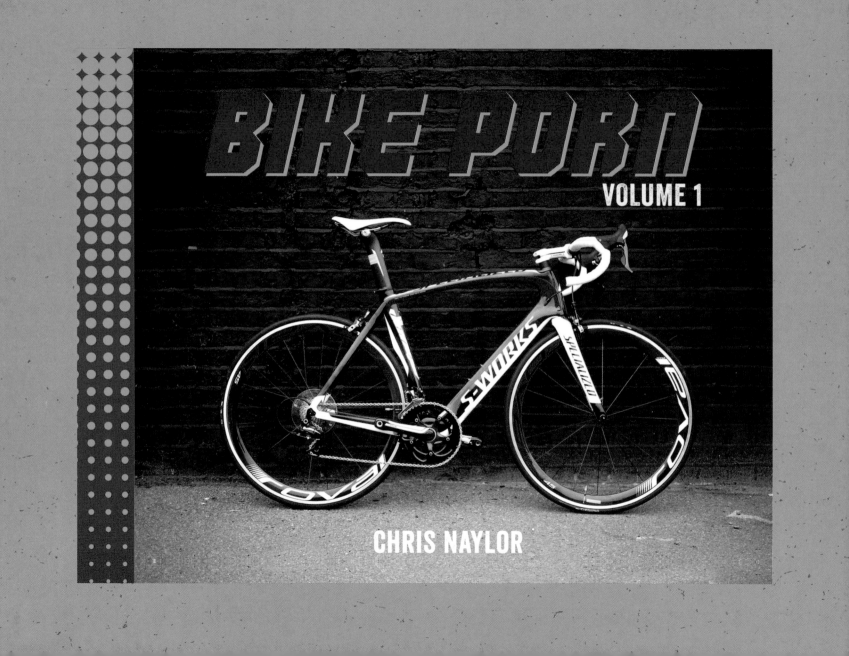

BIKE PORN

VOLUME 1

CHRIS NAYLOR

BIKE PORN

Chris Naylor

£14.99
Hardback
ISBN: 978-1-84953-481-9

All bikes are beautiful, but some are downright sexy.

BIKE PORN brings together stunning photographs of some of the most seductive and tantalising bikes ever made, from the slickest single-speeds to the most teched-out racing machines and beyond, captured in all their finely crafted glory.

If you're interested in finding out more about our books, find us on Facebook at Summersdale Publishers and follow us on Twitter at @Summersdale.

www.summersdale.com